"I'm teachin' PJ to write. What do we call this letter?"

"It's very clear and there aren't any clouds. Why can't
we see God up there?"

DOLLY HIT ME BACK!

by

Bil Keane

FAWCETT GOLD MEDAL • NEW YORK

DOLLY HIT ME BACK!

© 1975, 1976 The Register & Tribune Syndicate, Inc.
© 1979 The Register & Tribune Syndicate, Inc.

All rights reserved

Published by special arrangement with The Register & Tribune
Syndicate, Inc. by Fawcett Gold Medal Books, a unit of
CBS Publications, the Consumer Publishing Division of
CBS Inc.

ISBN: 0-449-14273-6

Printed in the United States of America

First Fawcett Gold Medal printing: November 1979

10   9   8   7   6   5   4   3   2

"I don't know why Mommy and Daddy ever let you into this family!"

"Do I have to CLEAN UP my room, Mommy,
or can I just neaten it a little?"

"Look, Mommy! We're wading!"

"Wanna help us fly our kite, Daddy?"

"I love me, I love me not . . ."

"Could I eat this yesterday?".

"Oooooh! The wind is ticklin' my tummy!"

"An echo is like hearing yourself in a mirror."

"Why can't I get the new clothes sometime
and let Billy wear my hand-me-ups?"

"Do sharks ever come up in bathtubs?"

"Let's pretend I'm getting married and you guys sing 'Here Comes the Prize.'"

"I was bringin' these home for you, Mommy, but they melted."

"He's not here, but I'm the BOY of the house."

"Will you promise to be quiet if I take you tennising with me?"

"In the wintertime I think ice cream men just turn into normal people."

"Birthday?" "September.23rd."
"What year?" "Every year."

"Mommy, at weddings, why do they say 'aw-ful wedded wife'?"

"Could we have the meat in a doggy bag, and the fish in a kittycat bag and the lettuce in a turtle bag and . . ."

"Doesn't your camera have fine tuning, Daddy?"

"Let's go over there, Mommy! That lady's givin' out free examples!"

"Be patient, PJ. You can have my popcicle when I'm through."

"Mommy, Goldie won't grow up to be a shark, will she?"

"Stop that noise, PJ! I need a little piece of quiet around here!"

"No, thank you."

"Why don't eggs have a tab you can pull?"

"It's just the soap — we won't need that."

"Betcha I'd sleep later if I didn't have to take an afternoon nap."

"Mommy, why don't you 'God bless me' when
I sneeze 'stead of sayin' 'Cover your mouth'?"

"Mommy's payin' me a quarter to do this.
How much are you gettin'?"

"I'm teachin' PJ to swing, but he can't learn to get off by himself."

"Sam's heart's in the right place, though, Daddy."

"If I put it under my pillow will the button fairy
bring me some money?"

"We didn't go to the seashore at all during the summer 'cause my mom went to see 'Jaws.'"

"Could I use some of your perfume, Mommy? I've got
a big favor to ask Daddy."

"Don't we have any RED apples? These are still yellow."

"See? He rows himself with his tail."

"Dolly called me a 'walking 'saster area.' Is that good or should I be mad?"

"Mommy likes to talk to her plants 'cause they never talk back."

"Daddy's shining his shoes with PJ!"

"I picked it out — Mommy just paid for it."

"My daddy said 'Is he here again?' and Mommy thinks you charge too much."

"If there wasn't so much JUNK in this drawer, I might be able to find the other half of my yo-yo."

"If you want me I'll be at Alan's or Scott's or Mark's or Todd's or Joey's."

"I can't take this note to my teacher, Mommy. You didn't leave enough margin."

"It was a pretty good party, 'cept there were GIRLS there."

"Daddies believe 'zactly what you say but mommies can read your mind."

"Which side of the toast do I butter?"

"Here you go, Mommy — I found you some hangers!"

"You sound tired, dear. Why don't you take a nap?"

"Mommy, will you light these so I can start practicing
for my birthday?"

"Kittycats only hear what they wanna hear, Jeffy."

"Do you want some peaches?" "No."
"No what?" "No peaches."

"The baby sitter last night said she'd never sit for us again."

"When we come out of school the lifeguard helps us across the street."

"Daddy showed me how to cut out paper persons."

"Why didn't they finish that bridge, Daddy?"

"We're talking to Grandma in stereo!"

"We flipped a coin — I said heads, Jeffy said tails, but it came up a building!"

"Hear that? Mommy says she's tired. Now we'll have to go to bed early."

"Grandma lets us help ourselves to as many as we want."

"The ones up front are the headlights. These are the footlights."

"I didn't do it, Mommy."

"Read slower, Daddy. I can't listen that fast."

"Okay, Scott, now hang up and let ME call YOU."

"Mommy, what year was PJ invented?"

"Will somebody deck up the cards so I can
serve 'em?"

"Because you're not a suitcase, that's why."

"I'm just washin' off my apple."

"Pretty soon we'll find out what kind of a face he has."

"I'll trade you this year — I'LL take the children around to the houses and YOU stay home and answer the confounded doorbell."

"That's our daddy. He's dressed as himself."

"Mommy's asleep but I'll play cards with you till she wakes up."

"Guess somebody must've fooled Mother Nature again."

"When the guy on TV did it all the dishes stayed on the table!"

"Mommy! Jeffy's just holdin' his hands NEAR the water!"

"Do I HAFTA look like Daddy when I grow up?"

"Mommy! I can get an autographed football if
we just go down to DG Home Center
and buy a color TV!"

"I lost a card from this deck but it doesn't matter 'cause it was only a two."

"I have the queen. The one I need is her hus-
band."

"Know what Grandma wears on her gold chain? Her glasses."

"Why does Sam need a license? He doesn't go fishing or hunting or get married or drive a car or . . ."

"Did you get the pictures we sent, Grandma? . . . And the gift? . . ."

"Ooops! Mommy! It's It's the wrong Grandma!"

"When they gather into a group like that, they're tellin' secrets!"

"Does it make any noise?"

"Aren't they goin' to have Thanksgiving this
year, Mommy?"

"How many stairs does this thing use up in a day?"

"All I'm gonna ask Santa for this year is a baby sister."

"There's nothing here for you."

"It costs too much for Mommy and Daddy to buy, but we'll ask Santa for it."

"Aw — it's another one marked 'Do Not Open Till Christmas.'"

" 'Twas the night before Christmas and all
through the house,
Not a mouse was s---, not a --- the creatures
were hung by the . . .
'Twas the night before Christmas and . . ."

"The Lanes put THEIR lights around the front
door and all their windows, across the
roof, over the chimney and . . ."

"Why did you say 'Yes, Virginia, there is a Santa Claus'? My name's Dolly, not Virginia."

" . . . and I got a frisbee for Aunt Nancy and
this harmonica for Grandma and . . ."

"What do I want, Mommy?"

"An old fashioned Christmas means like they had back in the sixties."

"They aren't REAL carolers, Mommy — one of them is Linda's mother."

"Can God give messages to Santa Claus?"

"I bought everybody's present 'cept one. What can I get for Daddy that costs 23 cents?"

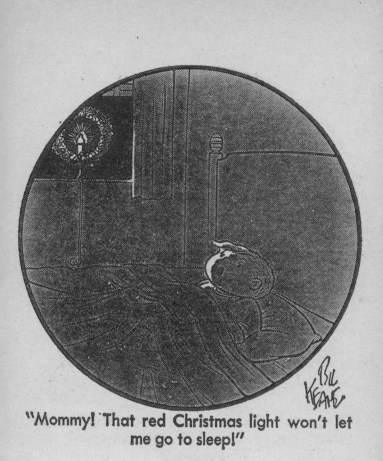

"Mommy! That red Christmas light won't let me go to sleep!"

"It's gettin' dark, Mommy! Guess we better get ready for bed before You-Know-Who comes!"

"Can we go outside and play with the boxes?"

"I'm goin' to bed early. I wanna be in good
shape to work on that new jigsaw
puzzle tomorrow."

"I guess it's just a little too much Christmas excitement."

"Boy, Grandma! I hope I can play with this and not have to wear it!"

"Already? Gee! We just put it UP!"

"Don't forget, Mommy! If we fall asleep, be
sure to wake us up at midnight!"

"Jeffy and PJ aren't startin' the New Year off right!"

"There's a different note in every hole."

"Is it anybody important?"

"I'm tryin' to remember, Mommy, but I can't think of it — what animal does meat loaf come from?"

"Wow! It's below nothing!"

"Watch out, Mommy! Don't step on the dragon!"

"Will you put my watch on so it's lookin' at me?"

"What would the little boy down the lane do with a bag of wool?"

"Did you know your hair was changin' color
down near your head?"

"Which toe did you hurt?"
"My thumb toe."

"When he sleeps he takes his head indoors."

"Hi, Mommy! Hint, hint!"

"I have to catch up on my diary. What did I do on January 2nd, 3rd, 4th, 5th, 6th, 7th and 8th?"

"I'm playin' my organ lady records to make
your plant happy so it'll grow."

"Mommy, if the McCauleys bring permission
slips, can they go skiing with us?"

"How many times have I told you not to talk
with your mouth full? Answer me!"

HAVE FUN WITH THE FAMILY CIRCUS

I'M TAKING A NAP   14144-6 $1.25

LOOK WHO'S HERE!   14207 $1.25

PEACE, MOMMY, PEACE   14145-4 $1.25

PEEKABOO! I LOVE YOU!   14174 $1.25

WANNA BE SMILED AT?   14118-7 $1.25

WHEN'S LATER, DADDY?   14124 $1.25

MINE   14056-3 $1.25

SMILE!   14172 $1.25

JEFFY'S LOOKIN' AT ME!   14096-2 $1.25

CAN I HAVE A COOKIE?   14155 $1.25

THE FAMILY CIRCUS   14068-7 $1.25

HELLO, GRANDMA?   14169 $1.25

I NEED A HUG   14147 $1.25

QUIET! MOMMY'S ASLEEP!   13930-1 $1.25

Buy them at your local bookstore or use this handy coupon for ordering.

COLUMBIA BOOK SERVICE (a CBS Publications Co.)
32275 Mally Road, P.O. Box FB, Madison Heights, MI 48071

Please send me the books I have checked above. Orders for less than 5 books must include 75¢ for the first book and 25¢ for each additional book to cover postage and handling. Orders for 5 books or more postage is FREE. Send check or money order only.

Cost $_____   Name _____

Postage_____   Address _____

Sales tax*_____   City _____

Total $_____   State _____ Zip _____

*The government requires us to collect sales tax in all states except AK, DE, MT, NH and OR.

This offer expires 3/13/81   8006-3